Heart Works

A Father's Grief

By Jerre Petersen

When you bury your child, you bury your dreams, your hopes, and your wishes.

I can honestly say that when Audrey died, I died along with her. She moved on to another world and I to another way of life consumed with grief.

I can only explain grief, if you have never experienced it, as the most painful disease, the slowest, most "maniacal" killer of the human heart.

Blessed are those who mourn

No matter what time it is, We are loved.

FOREWORD

I have to admit that I am not a writer. I am a scenic photographer. Late last summer, when needing assistance with a special project, I was referred by a mutual friend to Jerre Petersen. I found Jerre to be warm, competent, creative, and expressing a genuine eagerness to not only work with me on my current undertaking but to teach me ways to travel in heretofore unexplored territory for me - namely, computer marketing possibilities for my photography. He was generous in sharing his expertise, and our friendship was immediate; but something about Jerre bothered me. My senses told me he was deeply troubled about something. I didn't find out until later that he had suffered the loss of his daughter Audrey two and a half years before.

As our friendship grew, Jerre opened up more and shared with me some of the pain he was carrying in his heart. Some of this pain he had attempted to unburden in personal writings to and about Audrey, and I was permitted to share some of these. His words touched my soul, and I found myself in tears. From this man came beautiful expressions of the desperate feelings of a broken-hearted father, many of them reflecting my own experiences at the death of loved ones. When I asked him where he had learned to write like that, he told me he had not learned it, but that he felt the urgent need to write following the death of Audrey and couldn't not write. His writings are a gift - a gift to Jerre and to all who have suffered, especially those who have suffered the loss of a child.

I encouraged Jerre to put these writings in a book. I felt it would be a further loss if he didn't share the gift he had received, because his feelings are the feelings of many of us who have not found a way of expressing them.

Jerre also showed me some photographs he has taken since the death of his beautiful daughter, using photography, too, as an escape from his pain. Like the writings, he has been gifted in this with sensitivity and insightful expression. I have had the opportunity to see the work of hundreds of aspiring photographers, but Jerre has a way of capturing emotion that is rarely seen. There is a story in each photograph. In this book he has united the photographs with his writings. As you read and look, you can feel a presence.

At one point, Jerre confided to me that he wasn't sure he could do the book. I related to him that I had read about an old Indian way of finding answers to problems that had worked for me when I was at a professional crossroad. It was January, it was cold, and I was at the Painted Hills dressed only in my uniform of tee shirt, "Big Dog" shorts, and sandals. Drawing a circle in the sand, I stood in the middle of it and meditated. I don't know how long it took; but when, cold and shivering, I returned to my truck, I knew the solution to my dilemma. After Jerre heard this story, he in his own way also made a circle, found the answer, and this remarkable book is the result.

Sometimes we meet a person who can change lives. Jerre is one such person. I have learned a great deal from this man about life and healing. His gift of words and pictures will stay with the reader forever and perhaps provide greater fulfillment in life.

Who is he?

Jerre Arthur Petersen, Jr.   "A Father"

When Audrey died, words and feelings began to flow from my being, words which I had never realized were inside. A need to convey my love for her and to show others how important it is to love the children of the world has become my passion. I am just an ordinary man with regular goals, raising a small family, trying to make a business successful. I recognize that I have become different through this tragedy, and I believe with the sharing of my feelings, this book may be helpful for others who may unfortunately endure the tragedy of losing a loved one. I pray you never lose a child.

I have never really enjoyed the written word in the prior 42 years of my life, as I could honestly say I had not even read enough books to fill the digits on one hand. Since Audrey's death, I have read close to one hundred books. I just can't seem to get enough. My mind has always dreamed of better ways to do things. I have also wanted to be the best at what ever it is I do. I have an especially gifted heart when it comes to helping friends or someone in need. It is when I do these things I am overwhelmed with the most blessed feelings inside. It is then that I can just simply turn and walk away knowing I have been witness, thus rewarded. My heart has always led me through the life which I have known here on earth. I speak of being able to see with your heart many times in this book. Many times I have felt the magnificence of actually living it.

In January of 2002, I purchased a new camera. Although I had always been around photography and showed a liking for it, never had I considered anything I had done to be of exceptional quality.

I had been taking long walks throughout the city at all hours of the day. At times you may have seen me resting on the bank of a local river at 3 o'clock in the morning or running hard in the afternoon over a downtown bridge. These things I had to do for myself in the earliest days of grief. The days before she died, I started to write. I have bled on hundreds and hundreds of pages with my ink, recovering the thoughts that have poured through my mind. It has become a diary of love with words of pain.

I am the first to admit my literary faults; there are many. However, what has passed through my soul since April 5, 2000, could never be characterized by the written word.

This book in its entirety is mine and Audrey's. These are my writings. These are my photographs. These are my feelings. The design and typesetting I have quietly done by myself over these past months, days, and hours which have slowly trickled by since her death. I would say that the ideas have come to me in my dreams. I can only hope these dreams are possessed by Audrey herself.

I hope that as you read and look through this project of sadness, faith, and hope, you will be able to touch upon the love within yourself and to feel what it is that I can often now see with my heart.

I reside in Portland, Oregon, with my youngest daughter and my wife of 16 years.

We have maintained our faith in the Lord, and we continue to strengthen our relationships with friends and family.

Recently I met a very gentle man who had lost his own daughter when she was only 16 years of age, almost 40 years ago. He could not speak, the words which I could see in his eyes would just not come out. He merely acknowledged the common bond of pain which we now share throughout the motions of his aged body, then he quietly turned and walked away.

He quietly turned and walked away, as I have done myself so many times since the death of my Audrey.

Heart Works

A Father's Grief

Audrey Brianne Petersen, born on February 7th 1991 @ 4:50 am, died on April 5th 2000 @ 5:40 am. She danced with us for 9 years and 58 days. Left behind are her parents and a sister struggling with broken hearts along with a universe of questions for the heavens above.

I am Audrey's dad, Audrey's friend, Audrey's teacher, and Audrey's student. Today as I walk through the shadows of her death, I have learned to fear nothing.

For she has taught me this!

No matter what time it is, I am loved!

The Leaves Become The Richness Of The Earth

The Richness Of The Earth

Once a wind blew. A leaf, tattered and bent, fluttered with the flow of its breezes. The leaf danced and twirled like a windmill as she watched over the valley below. She felt droplets of rain from the heavens above. She felt warmth from the sun.

Below the valley grew closer each day. The leaf would wonder with desires. Often she wondered about the life beneath her.

Then one day without the whisper of a breeze, she sat admiring the beauty, the magnificence of her brothers and sisters which now covered the earth below, the rainbows of color which she now recognizes as her ancestors, ancestors of the wind, the trees, all eternity. She gently lets loose her holder; and like the grace of a butterfly, she softly drifts from one life to become another. She has become the richness of the earth.

We too are the richness of the earth.

Sadness

  At exactly 5:40 am on April 5th, 2000, she gently floated from this life into the next. Throughout the following pages I will share with you my ever changing life and what becomes of a father who has had to bury his child. This book is written for my Audrey as much as it is written for myself.
  For those who choose to read through these pages, I hope they become an education in how to share your love as well as how to accept it from others.

Solace

Seasons of Grief

I hope these words, woven with my images, become a source for healing throughout the process of any sadness that falls upon a human being. I have had many moments in this grief when all I wanted to do was plead for deliverance to the house of heaven where my daughter now resides. I have through the blood of my pen and the shutter of my camera found my own healing within. I can honestly say my prayers have been answered as I have learned throughout these seasons of grief where and to whom to turn. I have received love from strangers, I have been amazed by coincidences that would stagger anyone's imagination. These I find to be answers which have allowed me to become aware of my love for God. I pray this book branches out and touches the life of anyone who questions His existence.

Throughout the cold, bitter days of her illness, then death, I continued to search for miracles, sometimes finding myself going around in circles. Wandering around in circles is inevitable when your mind is weary with grief. The love inside an Audrey circle is never ending. Being here today by surviving the death of my child, I feel I am that miracle.

Seeking Miracles

Sunlight

Within the darkness of grief there will be days filled with sun.

Heaven came to me in the quiet of the night. As I lay there in the darkness, the tears flowed like rivers of the earth to cleanse my being. I felt whole again. She would speak to me. She would say that life in heaven is so wonderful, so colorful, so full of love, and she assured me that we would be together again; but most of all she told me that she was safe.

It is that one word "Safe" which has allowed me to move forward in my journey with this illness I speak of throughout this book as grief. We held each other's hands, we laughed again, we ran amongst the beauty of heaven, we felt each other's joys, we touched hearts again. Then for one last time she said, "I love you, Dad."

These words I hear softly and see often now with my heart.

These four words give me strength, encouraging me to live another day.

"I love you, Dad."
Four of the most beautiful words ever spoken.

For me Heaven is not a state of mind, it is an act of faith. I have always believed what we receive from the goodness of the earth is what we give back to her. When you can see with your heart you can truly experience her love. The value of life is only tangible in the sense of love.

Love is un-purchasable, love is never ending. You must learn to see with your heart, to feel with your soul. My Audrey had those gifts.

In many ways I really never felt she was mine, entirely mine, as I would thank God for her each and every day since the day she was born. I promised I would take good care of her. I always acknowledged that she belonged to the universe. I feel proud that the Lord had entrusted me to care for our angel. Angel Audrey.

From earth to eternity. Today my life is filled with silent memories and long, lingering days encrusted with the softness of her beauty, remembrance of a love which penetrated everyone and everything that came to pass her way. I do not know that I will ever be able to smile, to breathe, to smell, to hear or see the way that I once did. I am living, though, and I have come to recognize that life must move forward. With all the tears, the strains of breaths, I am slowly moving in that direction. After all, what choice do we really have? Live or Die.

"I love you, Audrey."

Swept Away

A woman in a white coat delivered words to me which swept away any reason. These words have haunted me continuously since those early morning hours when I heard, "Mr Petersen, she is gone now!" Will I one day be met by someone in a white coat who will speak of her arrival?

                I too am lost!

Bewildered

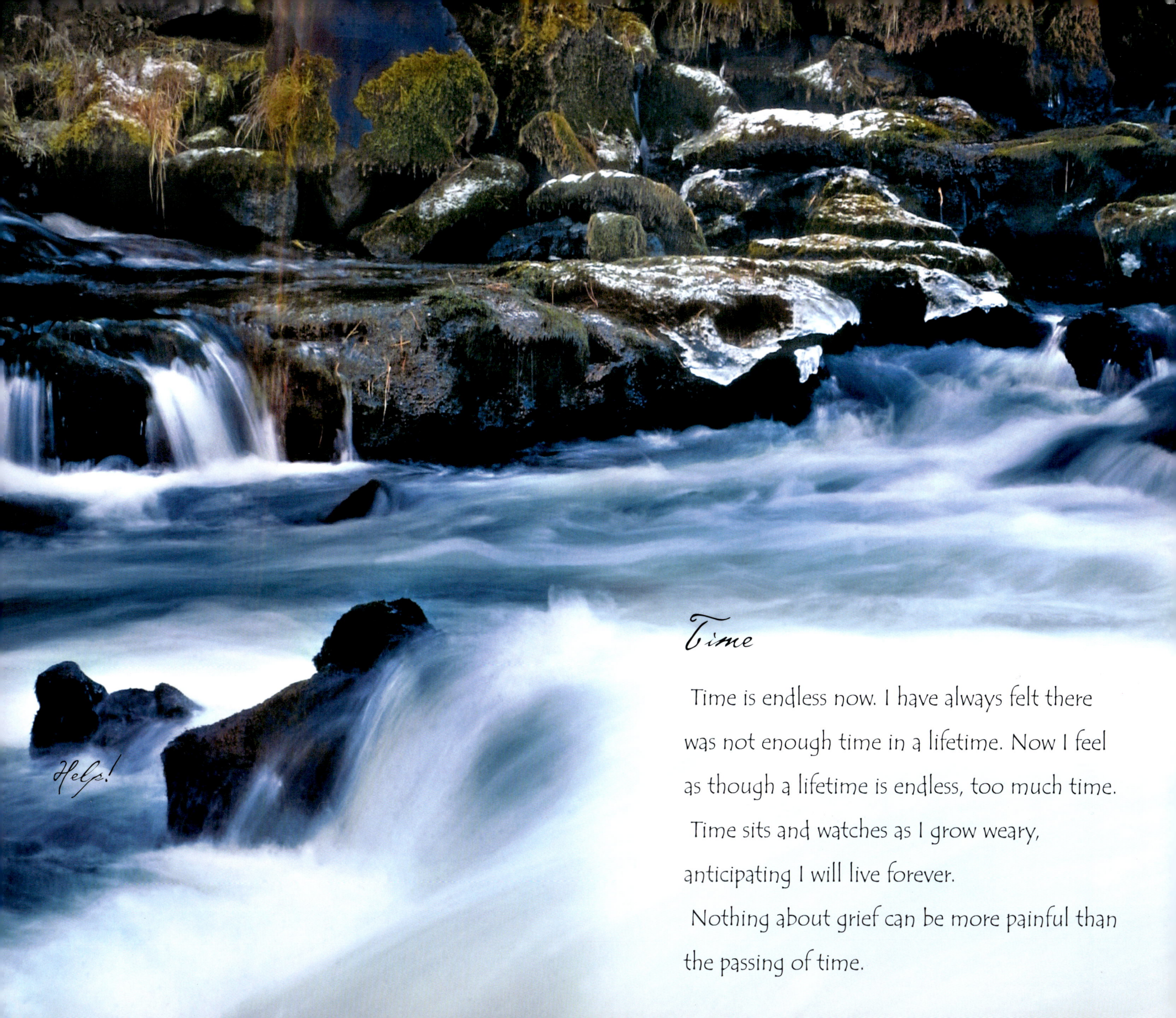

Help!

Time

Time is endless now. I have always felt there was not enough time in a lifetime. Now I feel as though a lifetime is endless, too much time.

Time sits and watches as I grow weary, anticipating I will live forever.

Nothing about grief can be more painful than the passing of time.

Abandoned

When she died I felt all alone, discouraged. My world became quiet. Since then I have stood still throughout the days, weathering the storms of grief.

I need to be with my pain.

I want to be alone.

Deserted

Weary

Although my structure remains standing amongst the desolate isolation I refer to as a father's grief, on the outside I still appear to have a foundation which can be rebuilt; on the inside the trusses of my soul are growing weaker.

Now I must rest.

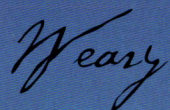

Moorings

Like a ship which has broken away from its mooring lines, I too feel as though I have run aground. It is here where I hope to spend the rest of my days withering in the middle of this grief. I have no needs, no wants, no desires other than to slowly melt away. To melt away into the earth.

Numb

Death

As I look across our land with these now swollen eyes, too often I am reminded there is someone with whom to share comfort in this grief. She, too, lies in pain. She is cold. With her endless reach, I am pulled towards her. She aches to be cleansed with my tears. She wants to feel my feet upon her tender soil, to hear my heart beat, to taste my words of sorrow. I am her friend. I have knelt upon her grace. I have shared many thoughts, so many emotions. I have come to realize there is only one thing with which to be truly confronted regarding life. Death.

Transition

When you hear the words, "I am sorry," while staring into the face of a dying child, you become cold and despondent. Amidst the ripples and the currents of all that has transpired since she has become ill, nothing has shaken my soul quite like these three words.

        I am sorry.

Dreary

Keepsakes

I have kept little things, like a lock of her hair which has the softness of a swift current in an undisturbed creek. In my backyard hangs a swing which lies motionless, reminding me time has stood still.

It is when I identify my loss through these thoughts, these things that I am able to again feel closer to her, I am able to breathe, if only for a moment.

Faces of Ash

It was Ash Wednesday that we received the news of our daughter's severe illness. Faces of ash roamed the halls of our affliction, the death march drummed its way through our ears until our hearts bled with an unconscionable misunderstanding that our daughter was going to die. A sea of ash penetrated the souls of all those who came to provide support for our family.

To my friends,
I am so sorry.

Views

I am eager to climb high upon any mountain, though I know what I am searching for may not be there. Still I must climb. When I have depleted myself of all energy, it is then that I am able to see beyond reality into the future. It is these tiny glimpses of sunlight into the future which bring me hope. Hope brings another opportunity to climb even higher.

    I can only hope she is there when I arrive.

Anticipation

Exploration

I have sat alone in the evenings wanting to reach out, to touch, to hear my favorite words of hers, "Hello, Dad." She leaves visions in my mind which span the oceans of our world. Some words are vague; still, somewhere in the distance, I hear a soft trace of her voice crying out for me to bring her home. I am left feeling helpless.

Searching

From Earth to Earth

Now I often wonder how the mother ocean may feel when she throws a wave up onto the shore. To have all her love spread out, never to return as a whole. To never again feel the love she once sheltered. The grief within has pounded its way onto my shore with questions of evolution.

Will I return again?

Protection

Running Wild

Audrey loved all the horses. Footsteps at my door are now only memories, like shadows of the sun. The melody of her voice, quiet days and lonely nights for now. She may be gone from my eyes; never will she be far from my mind. Perhaps in as little time as a day Audrey and I will run again.

   Run wild in a land of no pain.

Friendships

Fences

At times in our lives we may come upon a fence. A fence may sometimes speak harsh words. Keep out! I am now starting to recognize some of the most treasured memories I have obtained in my life. I value the friendships of those who have allowed me to wander beyond their fence line.

My Lord, today I am eager to journey beyond heaven's gates.

A Spirit Broken

I spent a summer on an uncle's farm, a completely different way of life than I was accustomed to living in a growing southern California city. A farm, for a child, unfolds a great deal of diversity in which a day is lived. There are chores, then more chores. No corner store to run off to for a soda in the heat of an afternoon. Everything seemed so different in comparison to how I had already been growing up. I began to love the farm life and certainly the animals. My uncle had several horses on his farm. They were corralled, as they were untame. I would often spend time watching their graceful beauty from the fence line. One day I felt an arm on my shoulder, and I heard the voice of my uncle speak of the spirit of an animal. He told me that when the spirit of an animal is broken, life is pretty much done.

He pointed out the elegance of a horse's eyes, how still with a tender firmness they would stare, beckoning the call of the warm sun to enlighten the life which lies deep in their soul; how the head reaches for the heavens to be brushed for encouragement before they soft shoe dance.

Then suddenly, the faintest of movements becomes a rage in an unharnessed passion to run.

He called this spirit, "Desire".

Maybe Tomorrow I will Run Again

Boundaries

There have been places in this grief in which I rolled out the fences, closed up the friendships, turned away a smile, shunned laughter, then forgotten I had done so. When I had awakened and had seen the growth around me, I came to realize the importance of these boundaries.

We need to spend time with our rage, our sadness, our loneliness. We need to drown in our tears. It is when we have done these things we can slowly take down the fences we have built and invite the world back into our lives. It is most important to take them down slowly, for death comes on quickly whereas grief lasts forever.

Understanding

Words

Words come and go; and although two words may be similar, the meaning is always different. I have learned on my journey through this sorrow that words bring comfort. Even words which may appear harsh are welcome in heartache. Perhaps it is harsh words filled with anger that ease the pain of this sadness more quickly than any other thing. I have heard the words, "You'll get over it." I have heard the words,

"You should be happy now that she is in heaven." I have disassembled these words which have come at me in the years following her death. I have created my own dictionary of their meanings. I have found that the power which is bestowed upon each and every word spoken is by far the most dangerous or the most kind weapon the human being will ever obtain. It is through the wisdom of grief I have found caution in my own vocabulary.

        Perhaps we all should.

Dust

The fine mist in the distance may bring a veil of hope for tomorrow, if only I see beyond then. I am now convinced that when all the dust has settled she will return. She must return like the sea. She has to.

Dust to dust.

Dismal

Mercy

It is a struggle from one day to the next, all the memories which return to pound away at the shell of your heart. Please do not blame me for the frailties I have gained since she has gone. Today my mind cannot react without memories. I cannot feel, breathe, see, hear, taste, touch, or smell without the thought of yesterday invading each moment of this new life,
yesterday which seems like ten thousand years ago today.

All the Mercy

Broken Hearted

Sparks Lake

In the beauty of Sparks Lake, creeks and streams flow silently, lovingly through the grasses of marsh to unite with all the crystal clear cool water which has refreshingly found its way there before. It all joins to become Sparks Lake, the most beautiful lake I have ever seen. I stop to photograph a memory for the future as a memory of the past unveils in all its fury the beauty of my eight-year-old daughter. I remember being here at this same place with her just a few years ago, I remember the joy in her heart as she ran and danced with her younger sister through these streams, I remember wiping her feet of the clear icy cold water that penetrated her beauty that day just three years before. I remember then thinking life couldn't be more perfect, how life was so wonderful, that I was so blessed, and how I was so proud to have two of the most beautiful girls in the universe. How lucky I was to be alive.

Today, I knelt in the beauty of Sparks Lake to add a few of my own drops of precious life to a body that would probably not have known the difference. Today, I know the difference. The difference is that my offerings contain enough love to fill the beauty of Sparks Lake many times over. The difference three years ago, which filled the veins, creeks and streams with life, brilliantly enlightening the reflections of Mt. Bachelor's beauty, allowing her "Sparks Lake" to be more beautiful than any other, was my Audrey. Audrey in the midst of it all. Today, I returned to nourish the ground with memories of her. Today, I have left behind the seeds of a life moving forward; tomorrow flowers will bloom. Then perhaps another child will dance and run within the beauty of this lake's soul, perhaps a child will hear the joy of a father's love without a word spoken, perhaps a body of water as beautiful as Sparks Lake will feel the tenderness of a memory and she will shine like she has never shined before.

Hope

Hope can mean many things in many ways in all sorts of situations. For a father who has buried his child, hope can appear to be lost. Today I have become the meaning of hope. I have related and I have acknowledged the power of love as well as hatred. I have felt fear, I have tasted illness. I have heard cries in the laughter of a young heart. I have looked beyond books for answers to the wrong which I have encountered. I have found amidst all that I have searched, no greater peace within than hope. Hope has leached its way throughout every vein of my life. Hope that soon I will hold her hand, smell her beauty, hear her words, splendor in her laughter, dance with her spirit. Hope today is my faith that tomorrow will bring another thought of her.

Lord, I hope you have heard my prayers.

Desire

Starting Over

Cries dance through my head as days turn from beautiful morning suns to clustered rainbows of gold. These visions shimmer in the life of a new day. I learn as each and every day unfolds our lives should not be taken lightly; they should be taken seriously, in the realm of all the order and disorder. Each life is a separate entity in the world of creation, infinite creation. It has taken this tragedy of death, the life of my child, to awaken the beauty which sleeps inside me. What I have learned in the last forty years of life cannot change what I remember just yesterday. I must drag myself through the torment of all these memories to be awakened by the beauty of a new day. Nothing seems more wonderful. Today my heart often aches for the beauty of the earth.

Sacrifice

Candles Burning

Dear Audrey, Tonight I lit a candle in your name so that you will not be forgotten in this world. Tonight is a tradition that started many years ago for the parents who have lost a loved one. Candles burn in each time zone throughout the world for a twenty-four hour period in remembrance of loved ones who have died. Tonight I sit and reflect on this event to put meaning to it. I rejoice momentarily, knowing the world is on fire with sadness for these loved ones. I cry for myself. Audrey, I feel shame sometimes in these tears, as I know you would want me to be stronger. I hope you understand these tears are only a defense in the wake of losing you. For it is when I cry that the memories feel more painful. There are times when I need to be in pain, feeling as though I deserve it for not being able to save your life. These years which have passed have allowed me to journey to places I thought I would never travel. I have seen life grow in places unimaginable. I have also seen death when it seemed impossible. In many ways I have kept to myself these past several years. I have struggled to not allow any life with happiness to come my way. Some of my friends have understood; others have just disappeared. Nevertheless, I am different, and now, so are they. As your candle burned tonight, Audrey, the candle within my heart burned brighter, enabling me to have a clearer vision of the future. At this hour my future looks good. I know it is you lighting the pathway ahead. With or without a candle, there will always be a place which burns brighter than anything, anywhere, anytime, in my heart for you.

It is 9:30 p.m., and u-r-loved.

Dad

Faith

 I gaze upon the river of memories and see amidst the flowing waters the diminishing events that unfolded at a time in my life in which I was not ready to swim the current, any current. Days passed slowly and nights seemed to grow longer without faith. Today I have faith that tomorrow I will emerge from this darkness of grief back into the life I knew before.

Seclusion

Tranquility

There have been moments when the tears of my sorrow have swallowed up the calm, peaceful beauty that surrounds me. When the storm has subsided, the feeling is often serene. I have learned that tears become loyal in their ability to rebuild the soul of a grieving father.

Harmony

Courage

I have been told courage will get me through this grief. To be brave. These are brash words from individuals who wear not my shoes. Silently in my mind I ask for them to be more compassionate, put themselves within my heart. The amount of strength it takes for me to get up in the morning to face another day. I buried my life when I buried my child. I have walked where those who pray, pray they never will. Today I am alive. Courage is for someone stepping through a line of fire to carry a comrade out on his shoulders, to breathe life into his dead lungs. Courage is for those who choose to enact it, then commit to it. It does not take courage to survive the death of a child. It is determination, strength, and weakness that will get me through this grief. Many times I have wanted to die with this sorrow. My love for life has become my weakness.

Weakness

Anguish

Torment

A day will come when the fury of grief will release itself.

Every feeling, every thought, every action will be in rhythm. All these emotions and some you thought you never had will release themselves in a torrent of rage. It is slowly after that you'll begin to heal, to start to live again.

A heart that bleeds with pain can learn to beat again.

Turmoil

The Storm

Among the sounds of nature, flashes of yesterday's life again invades my heart. Though the river may appear to be calm, underneath her gentle beauty she has fury. Today the river for me is cold and crisp. I sense another storm may be coming.

Father's Day *2 years after.*

Father's Day. I am awakened, nudged by a soft voice which seems to say, "Go find peace today, Dad, go find some peace within." Anniversaries can be so hard, dates to remember and joys relived. An anniversary waits with anticipation of a tear. This Father's Day I have filled another river in my life with more tears of sorrow.

It is the quietest day all year.

Sorrow

Dreams

In my dreams I have watched the world pass before my eyes, I have heard and understood the importance of these printed words, their meanings, and their ability to touch the hearts of others. I have been told within the heart of a human being there is recognition beyond what we hear, beyond what we are capable of seeing. I have learned that what we are capable of feeling in our heart is the greatest, most valuable experience to be obtained. It is when we have absorbed enough happiness, enough sadness, that we are capable of really loving. When we are capable of this kind of love, we are then capable of dying in peace.

    Today I feel as though I am ready to experience this peace.

Contentment

Distance

I have gone the distance. I have been from here to there, reenacting each and every moment of her life, each and every moment of her illness, and each and every moment of her death. I have gone the distance. My Lord, will you help me through the next pasture? Will you guide me beyond the next rainbow? Will you see that I make it home after my tiring journey?

        My Lord, I am so tired, as I have gone the distance.

Miles to go before I sleep

Morning Star

Often I will find myself contemplating the heavens above, being reminded of the spoken words to Abraham, "Look to the heavens above and you shall be blessed with as many children." These words, which had little meaning to me once, now lift the weight of sorrow from my shoulders, especially when I have awakened to the Morning Star. The brightest star of them all.

Contemplation

Chills

Two and one-half years after, I still tremble with a cold chill when I think about the transformation in my life. You were my everything.

You were my first born.

You have become the reason that I will rise again.

Serenity

Shadows

When the shadows come I may feel alone again. Everything around me seems to call your name. A soft breeze fluttering through the trees or a leaf dancing its way home.

I close my eyes to speak your name. Audrey, you are the wind, the rain, the sun on the cloudiest of days.

Munson Falls fairy princess

Balance

Patience

Today I am surrounded by a beauty I have not seen before. She calls me to walk amidst her grace, To enter her valley of enchantment.

I have been shown the value of patience. I have found peace amidst her tenderness. She has become my teacher. She is patient, waiting as I do in quiet contemplation for cries to be answered. Patient is a man engulfed in grief awaiting the sound of laughter.

Love is always patient.

Reflections

Among the reflections, all the memories which have passed since she died, I have learned many valuable lessons. The lessons learned have added value to my life, perhaps making me richer than I had ever imagined I would be. I would rather laugh anytime than cry. I would rather create than destroy. I would rather love than hate. I would rather live than die. Finally, most importantly, I have learned the importance of faith! Faith can only be obtained when you truly believe in something you may have once doubted.

Friendship

I have found throughout these years, days, months, hours, minutes and seconds that there is no greater treasure than the treasure of a friendship. It has been our friends who have held us together and shown us that life is still possible to live. Their kindness, their devotion to sit and listen and to just pass an hour of time with us allows the beautiful things around us to once again be visible. A friendship is one of God's greatest gifts.

River Of Life

There is a book I know of, a book of no words; a book which holds meanings beyond any word's explanation; a book so carefully illustrated, so extraordinarily knowledgeable it rests alone upon one shelf. This book resides deep within a heart, a book I reach for often in the days after her death. I have read within the letters of words, amongst the trillions of thoughts, that there is reason, that there is cause, that there will be again happiness. Faceless, nameless words drawn from the tip of my pen by way of my heart, words which say love can happen again, love will happen again.

These pages which encrust the words of my life have strengthened the soul of my being, allowing me to awaken each day to a new idea, a new thought of her.

Like a river which twists its way throughout a forest, this book of little words slowly trickles its way throughout the veins of my life. Today I am able to acknowledge feelings only obtainable through its words of love, its words of pain. My book of no words is slowly becoming the life of a father deep in grief. My book anticipates happiness, it wishes for hope, and it dreams of better tomorrows. I pray she is the one who has embedded these thoughts deep within my heart.

A river still full with life.

Questions

Shedding Tears

Did you not see me, Lord, that night she died? Did you not hear the words spoken from my heart? Had you not felt the anguish within me that quaked and rocked the universe? My Lord, I have shed enough tears to have filled all the great rivers of your earth. Has she fallen softly into your arms the way she once did with me, Lord? Do you speak of angel's hair, ice cream castles in the sky? Do you speak of flower fields at the end of every rainbow?

Crossing Over Eventually, we will all cross over a bridge in our lives that will change us from who we were into who we will become. The bridge may not span waters flowing rapidly or even have the beauty of wildlife nestling in for the spring around her structure; still in many ways the bridge in our minds can hold many of the same beauties and dangers as one which simply allows us to cross over a calm, flat river. "Careful," are the words I read, "do not cross; the river is high today; the bridge is shaky; it may not hold your weight; take responsibility for your own life." Do we take the opportunity to see what is on the other side of the bridge by ignoring the danger before us or do we stand back and look at the possibilities which exist in what may be gained by attempting to cross? Today, as I photograph another bridge in my life, I can see clearly that without trying I have gained nothing, and with nothing gained, I have lost. I have stood still, and another moment of possibility has quietly passed.

Right of Passage

There is a place in our hearts where we become bogged down, unable to move forward. It is written in the Bible, if you should pray from your heart, your prayer shall be given an answer. I have prayed for passage through this deep grief, I have prayed deeply from my heart. Today I am able to find other inlets through the sorrow of my rivers allowing me to move further down the stream of grief. Downstream where I have found the flat, calm, tranquil, soothing waters of a life moving forward.

Solitude

My Dearest Audrey,

I have encountered and endured pain beyond any imagination. I have reflected on goals and achievements. You were my greatest success. I have tormented the souls of the dead and most of the living. Questions of why? There are no words with which to describe the loss of you in my world today. Many quiet hours I have spent alone searching for you – just a glimpse! – then only to be disappointed with the turning of each corner. I am lost without you. Still I find the strength to go on because of you. Today I walk solemnly alone in the midst of needing you. Sweet Audrey, I pray tomorrow I will again be with you.

All my love, *Dad.*

Frozen

Time has stood still each moment since her illness. When the sun comes out, it tenderly melts away the grip of grief upon my heart, and life awakens again.
Today she watches over me
and I over her.
Let it shine.

Passion

Lessons

You have taught us how to enjoy life, how to embrace the outdoors. You have taught us how to listen for the singing of the birds, to smile when we hear a frog croak. You have taught us how to love, to give kindness, how to respect others. Most of all, you, Audrey, have taught us that no matter what time it is, we are loved.

We will never forget, we too will always love you.

Dementia

The places we go in our grief we could have never imagined. The other day I gave my youngest child a ride to school. On the way back, as I quietly meandered my way through this elegant old neighborhood, I came upon a house that stood out from all the others. Meticulously maintained, it appeared to belong somewhere else. Its lawns were lush and green, the edgings were all perfectly straight, and even the wrought iron fencing that lined the front and back yards was identically painted to match the trellis that hung over the porch. Thoughts started to race through my head over the lonely feelings I have inside regarding the loss of my Audrey. As I slowly passed beyond this home, I saw two young boys walking past on their way to school. I then saw this old man pass through his window, and one of the boys waved. He smiled back graciously, with a look of dignity; and still, from that distance, I could see the sadness in his eyes. I could almost feel it! It was at that moment that I could hear as crisply as a pin dropping in an old cement building, echoing throughout the vast voyages of space, one boy say to the other, "That is Mr. Petersen. He's lived here most of his life. I've chatted with him many times. Did you know that he had a little girl who died when she was very young? I don't think he has ever quite gotten over it. He speaks of her as though she were still with him. Once he showed me her picture. When I told him she looked just like an angel, he said, 'Yes she is, indeed, she is' and quietly, almost under his voice, I could hear him say, 'Daddy's little angel.'" These days I often reflect upon those beautiful nine years I had with Audrey and find myself sometimes creating a dementia that takes me into my later years, as though I am planning out how I will be dealing with my grief even 40 years from now.

Sensitivity

 A sensitive eye can catch the miracle of life within a valley of death. A sensitive eye may see colors in a world which can often appear to be black and white. A sensitive eye can inscribe a letter of beauty on the soul of a heart's saddened loss. A sensitive eye can see beyond tomorrow. A sensitive eye can hear the words in one single shaft of wheat. A sensitive eye hears the words,

"Hello, Dad."

Awareness

Doors

Having run into closed doors in this grief I have taken down my own "no solicitation" signs.

Tomorrow someone may enter who is capable of lifting the sadness from my heart, if only for a moment.

Welcome stranger.

The Wake

In the beginning we received lots of cards, hugs, handshakes, especially words of encouragement. Soon they start to all disappear. They vanish almost as quickly as they come. Then we are left alone to deal with all our emotions. This is the hardest of all the hurdles, for the beginning of grief comes with great pain. It does get easier. Still, in the beginning, time seems endless. I tell myself over and over it is okay for a man to cry. I shed lots of tears. I doubt they will ever go away. Maybe the tears are gifts from the heavens to drown the fires in my soul. Memories: we have to learn to enjoy them with song and sorrow. Most days in the beginning feel like hell - you just want to burn in it. Then light shines a pathway through your corridor of grief which allows you to see again, even if only momentarily. I have learned to keep my hands busy. Today I write. Writing for me has become a work of love. I feel as if this will become my legacy, for with each word I write I can see again, seeing things in this world that I have never seen before. Sometimes I smile when I read what I have written. The smiles tend to change to laughter. Laughter cures my broken heart, if only for a moment. With one change comes another. Today I sit and listen to her music. I'll sit and just listen to the sounds that once made her smile. Sometimes I cry. Sometimes I can feel her wiping the wet shadows from my eyes. I fall asleep. I dream of her. Today I taste the magnificent beauty of Audrey. By being in thought of her, I can touch upon the marvelous wisdom she has bestowed upon us. Today I am living better, I am loving more. In the wake of all that has transpired during these last two and one-half years, I can honestly say I have become a better person. Grief works in strange ways, for it has carefully slowed me down enough, allowing me to acknowledge the value of a human life and the relationships we keep well above the quality of them. I have walked a tightrope within the essence of time passed. I believe I have also found the key to life and the beauty or ugliness we may receive from it within two simple and basic approaches. Learn to ask for forgiveness as well as to be able to forgive. My Lord, I ask for your forgiveness of my wild cries in the night. My Lord, today I am able to forgive you for not saving her life.

There are days that I sit and stare into the reflections of a pond in my own backyard, and the memories of the last ten years of my life unfold before my eyes, starting from the day that she was born, and sadly, ending the day that she took her last breaths of life. My daughter Audrey Brianne died just fifteen months ago of an incurable, inoperable brain tumor, which took her life in twenty-seven days from the day she was diagnosed. She was only nine years old. The past fifteen months of my own life have been consumed by the grief that has followed that dreadful day. I have been asked almost continuously from that day forward how I am doing. In this world there are many more individuals who have faced the same sorrowful road that I am now journeying, undoubtedly all finding their own ways to grieve. Grief comes naturally to someone caught smack in the middle of it. There is no proper way to grieve. Grief comes in stages that may last for weeks and years, a lifetime. Grief never goes away; it only gets easier.

Almost within days of her death, I started to dig holes in my backyard. I suppose I was in need of digging my way to the devil. I had to blame someone for this tragedy. He was the obvious choice, so I dug with a passion, that when I finally reached him, I would destroy him so that he would never cause anyone else the anguish I was living through. As the weeks passed and the holes became larger and larger, I started to hear a voice inside my head that insisted I look elsewhere. The devil was not within reach by shovel and hard labor. I would only be able to achieve my meeting with him through mind, body, and soul. With the persistent mental and physical energy that I had been putting into the depth and breadth of these holes, I had crushed the last breath of evil from my spirit. At this point I started to realize that within every human being is the answer to any question or problem we have. We only need to take time to listen, to hear with our hearts and not our ears, and to see with our hearts and not our eyes. I was slowly becoming the man that perhaps I was meant to be all along. I started to listen harder, to feel.

The fast pace of life meant nothing any more. There is a story in the Bible that speaks of a man who shed and discarded all the riches and lavish ways of life that he had built for himself and family once he had learned of the illness of his young son. Seven days later the young boy died, and the man resumed the way he had once lived before this tragedy occurred. Being continually asked by so many people why he was back to wearing all the riches and once again living lavishly, his simple reply was, life must go on. Unlike King David, I have not found the ease of slipping back into a life that I once had, nor do I care to. Golf on the weekends, trips on the river, or fishing with a few friends seem to be on hold these days, as I now enjoy spending time alone or with a different set of friends studying ancient history and building my spiritual and Christian foundation that will one day allow me to be with her again.

I have cried so long and so deeply that I've needed to gasp into the lowest cavities of my lungs to take the last breath of air that would sustain my life only until the next wave of loneliness or the next horrible memory of her illness would come again. Having crawled into the darkest places to be all alone where I could yell at my God has given me the ability to live beyond tomorrow. Gaining the knowledge throughout the hardships of losing a child, the greatest tragedy that anyone could ever live with, has enabled me to see the world through a different set of eyes.

A man's grief is just that. We all grieve differently. We are all created differently. The thoughts, the actions, and the ways in which we live before and after the loss of a loved one are ours all alone. Grief is there to keep us busy when we are in need of something to do. It's there to help with all the anger, there to help shed tears, there to help with everything that will happen and become of us in our future. Then when we have learned to change a little grief into a little love, the cycle starts all over again.

The more that we deal with the grief, the less the pain is and the easier our lives are, and the memories become more like treasures than daggers. Now as I sit and gaze beyond the reflections of her ponds, seeing her fish that once swam in an aquarium enjoying the larger mass of water to live in, I can compare my world to the heavens and to the reality that there is so much more beyond this life.

Gaining new friendships by being the father of a dead child sustains the way in which I now live and has given me the need to share a few lessons that I have learned with those who can't show any compassion toward a friend or family member who has lost a loved one. Never tell someone who has lost a loved one that there is no such thing as God or heaven. Never say, "I know how you must feel." Everyone's grief is different. Never disappear or avoid the person that has had the loss. Let your friends or family members talk about their loss. Ask questions about what happened. You'll be surprised how much you'll learn and how much they may want to share. Just because someone has died doesn't mean they're to be forgotten. Never be ashamed of crying; tears are one of the greatest gifts we all have. They're signals to those around us that we have feelings and that we care, that we are capable of a little love and compassion. Send a card, make a phone call.

Audrey's fish that once lived in an aquarium, and according to the experts, was not supposed to live in an outdoor environment and among the Koi fish, has grown five times its size in just over a year. As I look into the clear waters and see the beauty of this magnificent and colorful fish, I am overwhelmed with happiness, as though I can hear her say, "Dad, I am OK." Life goes on. Today I am living proof of that.

For those of you who have been enduring the same trials and tribulations through your own loss, I would encourage you to take these changes and make the very best of what you can of them. The pain, hurt, and loneliness may never go away. I have spent many hours on long walks, looking at the beautiful gift of life that the Northwest has to offer. I believe this is God's Picasso. Breathe slow, deep breaths; the slower you breathe, the more relaxed you'll become and the more in touch you'll be with your emotions. That is when you'll be able to think between the memories of the years with your loved one and enjoy them. Write down everything about your thoughts and the little gifts that they send you. You'll soon find a love for writing. Perhaps your writing will become your legacy. Listen to their favorite music, cook their favorite meal, and savor each and every bite of it. Find in these things what they enjoyed the most and enjoy it yourself. On a balloon, write them a love note and watch it float away gracefully. Plant their favorite flower in the backyard and watch it grow magnificently. Quietly talk with them; they will hear you.

In all, in the passing of the last several years, I have felt guilt; I have had incredible anger; watched friends slip into the darkness; become spiritual; and, most importantly, learned to love. The greatest of all the reflections I see today are the reminders that life goes on. The sad, lonely feelings will always be there as a reminder that tomorrow I will be in a land of beauty with no hate and no pain; and that's when the smile that overwhelms my being reminds me of her in a better way.

U-r-loved, *Audrey's Dad.*

Empty

Without

 In the beginning I planted myself on my knees to inquire within and outside myself what it is that I could do without. All the monies, everything I own, anything I have ever obtained I would most surely trade, yes, go without for the life of my child. I have gained respect from those who have watched me endure these years of grief. Their words which say so often with silence: "Look at what you have gone without." Without my Audrey I have truly understood the meaning of being without.

Dear Audrey,

Today I thought a lot about what I would want to write to you. I thought I would write about darkness. What would I say to you about a light that shines within my soul, enlightening a path where I might see a way that leads me back to you. Today, Audrey, I am blind. There is a darkness in my world where I haven't journeyed before. A darkness in which I have not been educated. A darkness that I must find my way out of by myself before I can see clearly again; before I can live again. I have to admit, Audrey, that I never anticipated my being blind would have an advantage over those who can see. It is in this darkness, this inability to utilize my eyes, that I start to acknowledge my other senses; that I begin to understand the reason we are given these senses. Never having seen you, I gently place my hands upon your flesh. I meander throughout the softness of your structure to realize that I am climbing the highest mountain so, when I have accomplished its height, I might see the world below me: the world in all its beauty and all its ugliness. It is then that I realize I have a purpose. In this realization of my purpose, I ponder. Within these thoughts I recognize that I am above everything. Being above everything I understand my ability to obtain. Audrey, I have a question! By being above everything and having the ability to obtain anything, what is it that you would think I would want? Today, Audrey, I closed my eyes and I saw you. In my selfishness to obtain and to have anything, I placed my hands once again upon your face, where I felt your beautiful smile again. It is there that I tasted your tears; it is there that I realized and enjoyed the fragrance of your flowing brown hair; it is there that I danced for a moment, where I laughed again. Having only seen you for the short period of your life is better than having never seen you at all. I have climbed higher than I ever thought I would climb for the privilege of really understanding these words. By being blind today, Audrey, I will forever be able to see you in my heart.

What is in the heart, I have learned, lasts forever. This I find to be the true meaning of a life.

What is in the heart lasts forever! *All my love, Dad.*

Whirlwind

Like nothing I have ever encountered, the speed of time passed has been a blur. Little time to do anything other than to watch a child die before your eyes. She passed into the depths of what we are left with as parents, grief. I have been through these depths. I, too, am dizzy with questions, certainly too tired to make sense of any explanations. I have struggled, I have conquered, and I have found some hope within a battered heart. With time we all do. From time to time she comes back to me to remind me of our bond - the bond till I, too, shall die. The bond of love which is never ending. Grief continues from one whirlwind moment until the next. *Today I would rather dance. Would anyone care to dance?*

Turbulence

God, grant me the serenity to accept the things I cannot change,

courage to change the things I can, and the wisdom to know the difference.

Amen.

Tears

With the purity of our tears God, too, becomes richer. Richer with the hearts and souls of all those who pass before Him. God also sheds tears. Together we cleanse the earth.

Amen

We too are The Richness Of The Earth.

In Memory: *Audrey Brianne Petersen*

Thanks to:
Chérie Elizabeth Petersen, Julie Saltamachio Petersen, Kari Ann Kather, Rod Liske, Jerry and Ann Hunt, Joe and Teri Wehage, Don and Melinda Olson, Gene Zimmerman, Leah Saltamachio Peters, Jeff Peters, Mary Saltamachio Spencer, Ronald Dey, Pete and Beverly Saltamachio, Beth Saltamachio Barg, Mom, Dad, and my sister Heidi.
Father Robert Barricks, Father John Amsberry, the students, faculty, friends and parishioners of Holy Family Catholic Church of Portland, Oregon.
Truly you are some of the kindest human beings to live on God's earth. Your support, love and kindness to the Petersen Family has been by far some of the most compassionate behavior one could be honored with in a lifetime. Too many to mention all your names, surely they would fill the pages of this book. So let me just say, from the deepest part of my heart,

    "U R Loved."

Along my journey I have made the acquaintance of many understanding, compassionate individuals who have stood out from most of the others.
One such individual is Oregon photographer Jerry Hunt. I am grateful for the friendship which the Lord has bestowed upon me, introducing me to Jerry in late August of 2002.
Jerry's beautiful scenic photography has inspired me to review my own work and to take it many steps further. His kindness and words of encouragement allowed me to move forward throughout this project. I am very honest in saying without the friendship of someone whom I jokingly call Pops, old man, grandpa, old dog, and now Dad, I do not believe I could have finished this endeavor. "Thank you Jerry."
I am also graced by the magnificent foreword with which Jerry has gifted me. Ann Hunt, Jerry's wife, whom I also refer to as Mom, you are a very special lady with a gigantic heart. I love you both.

A very special thank you to my wife, Julie Saltamachio Petersen. Thank you for our girls and for your support.

The printing mastery of this book is achieved by Dynagraphics of Portland Oregon, with special thanks to my little brother, Rod Liske.

Text Copyright © 2003 Heart-Work-Publishing

Photographic Copyright © 2003 Heart-Work-Publishing

Jerre Petersen
Design, Photography, Text.